Berit Hildre

Modelling
HEADS AND FACES

A & C Black

First published in 2005 by
Ulisse Editions
15, rue Mansart
75009 Paris, France

First published in English in 2008 by
A&C Black Publishers
50 Bedford Square
London WC1B 3DP
www.acblack.com

ISBN 978 1 4081 0267 1
Reprinted 2012

Translation by Niccola Shearman

Cover design by James Watson

Printed in China by C&C Offset Printing Co., Ltd

Contents

Beginning of a Friendship, *1999, fired and waxed clay, h: 35cm.*

*I*ntroduction

The first task given to every new student in my classes is to model a head. The reasons for this are numerous. The human head presents the opportunity to study convex and concave surfaces as well as detail from a 'familiar' and readily-available subject: one we believe we know and yet which, with the best will and all the materials in the world, we are unable to reproduce exactly. Without exception, all students observe their fellow humans with a keener gaze after this first lesson; they study cheek bones, eyes and jaws in a continual search for information. If the eyes are the mirror to the soul, then the face is the mirror to the emotions. A face betrays everything. It is the reflection of our mood, whether we like it or not. The deepest currents of our character, the tiniest changes in temperament, even suppressed emotions; they all make their impression on our face. And indeed, our face continues to communicate when words fail. The brightness of a particular face invites closer study, and even more so when this quality can be captured for ever by 'translating' it into another material, allowing us to engage further with it whenever we choose.

Feelings overcome us, unavoidably and unintentionally. They deliver us up to others and at the same time others to us, revealing a vast field of communication deep within each person. Faces communicate, so to speak, from soul to soul. The opportunities to follow these paths of emotional exchange are rare and often missed. Artworks give us the chance both to encounter others and to recognise our own selves, to fuse one with the other; even perhaps the chance to encounter something of the essence of being.

All of this convinces me that everyone, even the uninitiated, can spend hours absorbed in the creation of a head. It is a question of working on bringing that 'certain something' to the fore, even if initially the difficulties are great and the hands unskilled. Later, once one has mastered a few of the effective basic techniques, the sculpting of a head will always remain the hardest but also the most satisfying stage of creation. The challenge is to concentrate the entire personality of a figure on this small surface area. An expressionless, empty face can 'kill' the whole work and make it completely unappealing, just as a limp body with a pinched face can have an equally devastating effect. The head, body and limbs should all combine to express the same overall character, and to transmit the same feelings. It is in this subtle transference of such separate elements that the secrets lie which can occupy many an artist for his or her whole life. And the best-kept secrets are the most enduring.

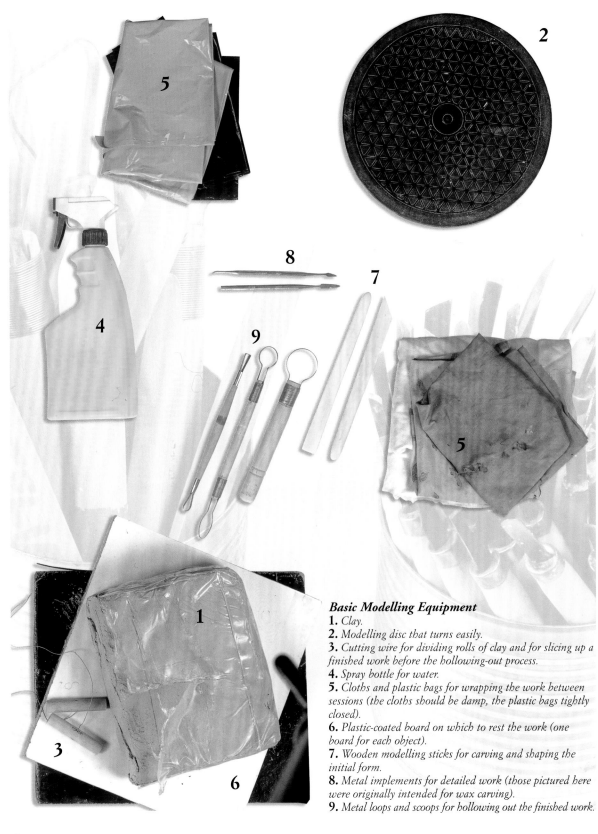

Basic Modelling Equipment

1. *Clay.*

2. *Modelling disc that turns easily.*

3. *Cutting wire for dividing rolls of clay and for slicing up a finished work before the hollowing-out process.*

4. *Spray bottle for water.*

5. *Cloths and plastic bags for wrapping the work between sessions (the cloths should be damp, the plastic bags tightly closed).*

6. *Plastic-coated board on which to rest the work (one board for each object).*

7. *Wooden modelling sticks for carving and shaping the initial form.*

8. *Metal implements for detailed work (those pictured here were originally intended for wax carving).*

9. *Metal loops and scoops for hollowing out the finished work.*

1 *The Tools, the Clay*

In this book only small attention will be paid to the basics of clay modelling. Nonetheless, I would like to summarise some general aspects of the technique.

The Clay

You should work exclusively with blended (or grogged) clay. The unblended variety has a very pleasant feel to it, but is unsuitable for strong-walled structures. The addition of grog (finely-ground particles of fired clay) results in a clay body that is less sticky and better suited to building up large pieces. With the extra benefits of reduced shrinkage and cracking, the finished works are less vulnerable during the drying-out and firing processes. Clay is not especially expensive and can be bought in ready-to-use bags from ceramic suppliers, where there will be a range of different bodies on offer, each with varying amounts and grades of added grog. I personally work with a raku body containing 40% grog in a particle size of 0–2 mm.

Ask to see different examples in order to decide upon your preferred material, but always remember that the greater the proportion and particle-size of grog in the clay, the fewer problems you will encounter during the drying and firing of the finished pieces.

Example of a stoneware body with 40% grog in a particle sizeof 0–2 mm.

Tip: For work on fine details, follow the process shown below in order to obtain a small amount of smooth clay free of coarse particles.

Take a small ball of clay and knock it firmly on a hard surface.

You can then scrape off a fine grog-free surface layer.

Young Woman Squatting, *2000, fired and waxed clay, h: 27cm.*

When opening a fresh bag of clay, you will find it ready compacted and not requiring any kneading. However, any lumps of clay prepared from scraps of unused or left-over material will need to be thoroughly beaten with a wooden bat in order to drive out any trapped air bubbles.

The tools

Your basic equipment should include a wooden modelling stick and one or two metal implements with flat blades for working in the details (if these are not readily available, any other small metal tool can be adapted for the purpose). These will be adequate to begin with. Hands are always the best tool for the initial building stage, after which the wooden stick can be used to mould the clay and create the overall form. The latter is too thick and clumsy for the later detailing stage, for which you will need to employ your finer tools. Thumbs are of course always useful, but avoid smoothing the work too much with the fingers, as this can easily erase fine detailing and give the work a 'watered down' look. A cutting wire can be used to slice workable amounts of clay off a large block, and for cutting up the finished work for the hollowing-out process.

Your essential equipment will also include a supply of cloths and plastic bags, a rotating disc, coated boards (one for each object), a bottle for spraying water, a sculptor's pedestal, a mirror, and a 'data base' of images, books and anatomical diagrams.

Storing the work

A plastic bucket with a lid is recommended for the storage of large masses of clay. Protect the object you are working on between each session by wrapping it in damp cloths and sealing the whole in a plastic bag. Above all, do not moisten the work too much! It is not a question of drenching the piece, but rather of retaining the clay's original moisture. A work that is too wet becomes sticky or – far worse – can soften up and fall apart. For this reason it is advisable to dampen the cloths rather than the clay itself. Always close the bag tightly with string or sticky tape. As long as no air can enter then the clay cannot dry out. If, in spite of all this, you should find your piece is too dry, then you can roughen the surface and re-apply damp cloths to the affected parts.

This will soon restore the clay to a workable state. A work of medium size is best stored in a large plastic dustbin bag, as in the picture below.

Work standing up!

For this a sculptor's pedestal is indispensable. Standing up makes you more flexible and more alert. But remember to allow yourself breaks: do not overestimate your powers of concentration. You will find that an intensive and fruitful session can pass in no time, while on the other hand you may spend hours working on fine details and going over mistakes, often with unsuccessful or even catastrophic results. There are no hard and fast rules here, except to ensure that you are concentrating throughout your session. You may of course sit down for detailed work.

Place your work in a plastic sack and keep this airtight by closing with a clothes peg or a rubber band.

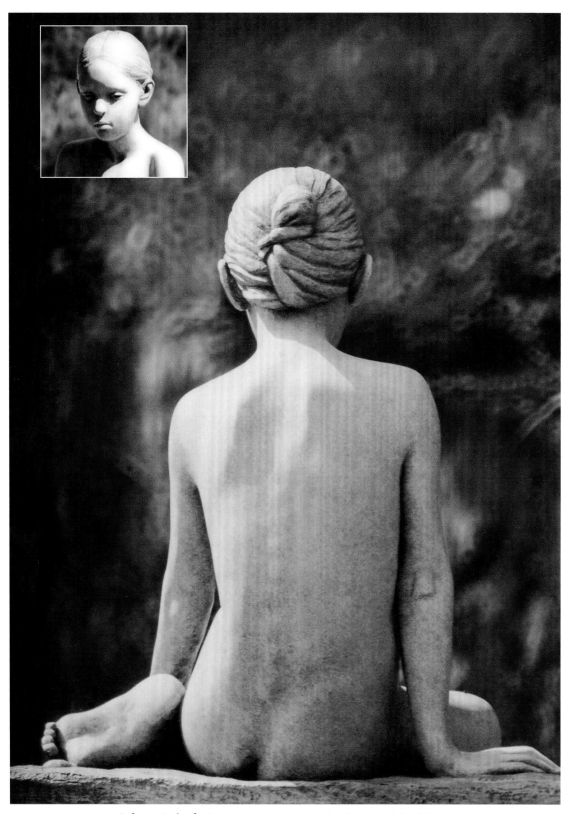

Rebecca isn't playing any more, 1999, *fired and patinated clay, life-size.*

2 Anatomy of the Head and Neck

Some people may find anatomical studies daunting. However, once you have become acquainted with the most important (visible) bones and (superficial) muscles, these will soon form the main points of reference for your work. The bone structure is the same in every human being, just as we all have the same muscles, in the same places, only more or less pronounced.

Anatomy provides the foundation for our art form: a solid reference; measurable and reliable. It is the written score which later allows us to apply our own personal interpretation or structured improvisation. For we have to know a subject really well before we can attempt to reproduce it. How often have I heard the complaint, 'The ears are so difficult!' In fact, it is not especially difficult to model an ear. If one is unfamiliar with it, perhaps; if it has not been observed closely, then most definitely. Once you have studied and sculpted a few ears, examining each small detail; then you will understand that most difficulties arise simply as a result of unfamiliarity.

Remember: It is no more difficult to learn to model a particular part of the face than it is to ride a bike. It takes a while, but with time the whole process comes so naturally that one forgets ever having to learn it in the first place.

The skull

We will start our observations with the bones of the skull. The idea is not to undertake an advanced anatomy session, but simply to concentrate on the most important aspects. The skull is fundamentally an ovoid; in

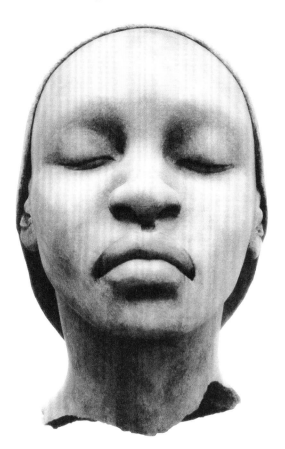

Vestige, *1998, fired and patinated clay, h: 52cm.*

other words, egg shaped. It consists of two main areas: the cranium (skull); and the facial bones (face).

The cranium

This consists of seven individual bones, attached firmly to each other by fine seams. The view from above clearly shows the egg-shaped form which the skull takes, narrowing towards the front and widening again at the ears, to finish in a rounded form at the back.

The facial bones

These bones, which protect the sense organs, are arranged in symmetrical pairs. The part generally known as the jaw in fact consists of the upper jaw (or maxilla) and the lower jaw (mandible), the latter being the largest bone in the face, and the only one which moves. In order to model a realistic head, one must first take into account the overall proportions of the skull, before observing closely the following areas:

The eye sockets:

Notice their angular, gently rounded form, a little like sunglasses. The eyebrow forms the upper edge, standing out over the lower edge, and generally protruding further in men than in women. To the side of the eye sockets are the temple hollows, usually known simply as the temples.

The cheek bones:

The anatomical name for this raised and generally quite

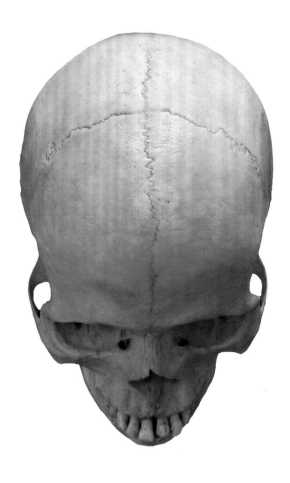

pronounced bone is the zygomatic, while the fine curve that leads to the ear is known as the zygomatic arch. In some people, the jaw appears wider than the cheek bones, and this is usually due to well-developed chewing muscles. The three-quarter view shows a depression between the eye socket and the cheekbone. (NB: this is an important reference point and will come up again later, under discussion of the 'three-quarter test'). The cheekbone has particular significance to the sculpting of a face. For the fundamental shape of the face – whether oval or square – depends upon the degree to which the cheekbones stand out. The most common mistake consists in setting the cheekbones too close to the eye sockets and too far towards the centre of the face.

The chin:
When viewed from below, the lower jaw – or chin – takes the shape of a horseshoe which straightens off towards the front. The jaw joint lies directly in front of the ear. A man's lower jaw is both larger and more angular; a woman's more rounded. Take care not to position the curve of the jaw behind the ear.

General points
The female skull is flatter than the male, with a steeper forehead and a less pronounced zygotic arch. When starting out, always keep an anatomical diagram to hand, and study it carefully each time you begin working on a head. Use yourself as a model too: hold up a mirror and touch your forehead, running your fingers over the eye sockets, the temples, the cheek bones and the jaw, finishing at the earlobes.

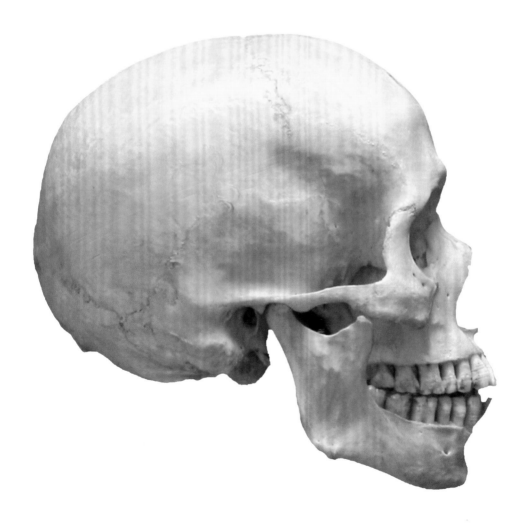

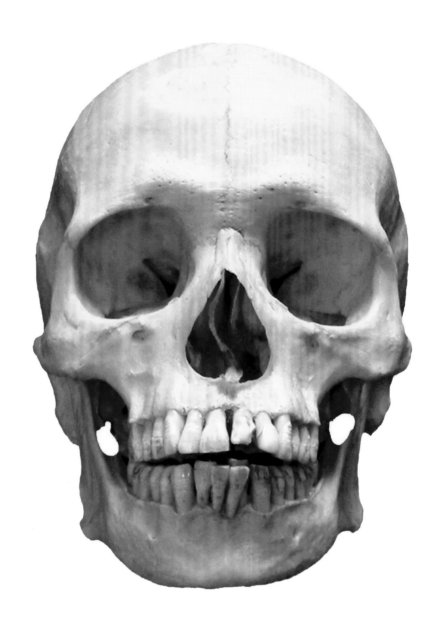

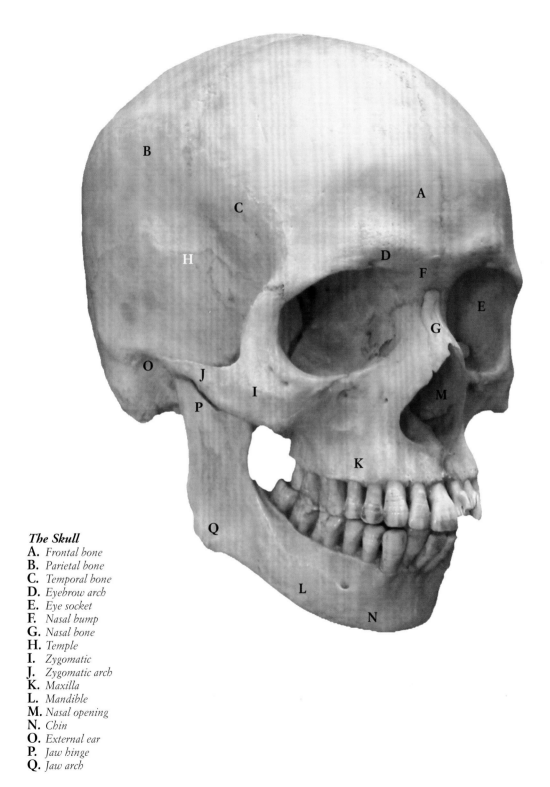

The Skull
A. *Frontal bone*
B. *Parietal bone*
C. *Temporal bone*
D. *Eyebrow arch*
E. *Eye socket*
F. *Nasal bump*
G. *Nasal bone*
H. *Temple*
I. *Zygomatic*
J. *Zygomatic arch*
K. *Maxilla*
L. *Mandible*
M. *Nasal opening*
N. *Chin*
O. *External ear*
P. *Jaw hinge*
Q. *Jaw arch*

The shoulder girdle

If you wish to model a bust then you will need to get to know the proportions of the neck and shoulder girdle. The latter structure consists of the shoulder blades, the collar bones and the breast bone (sternum). It links the upper extremities of the body to the trunk, and can be compared in shape to a rhombus. The cervical vertebrae sit at the centre and slightly to the front of this rhomboid structure.

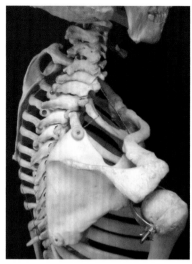

Side view of the shoulder girdle.

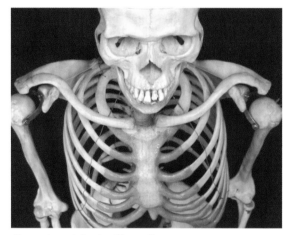

Front view of the shoulder girdle.

The neck

The neck is like a cylinder inserted into the shoulder girdle, and leaning gently forwards over the torso. In women the neck tends to be longer, while the more pronounced trapezoid muscles in men make their necks appear shorter and more solid. For the sake of clarity we will divide the neck into three sections: the neck extensor muscles; the trapezoids, and the throat.

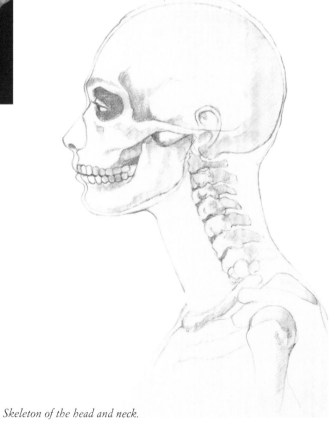

Skeleton of the head and neck.

16

The Neck Extensor
(musculus sternocleidomastoideus)

You will soon be on familiar terms with this muscle of the unpronounceable name. It stands out noticeably and is immediately visible whenever we turn our heads. It connects the skull to the clavicle (collar bone) and the sternum, and attaches to the lower temporal bone just behind the ear; to the curved occipital bone at the base of the skull, and at its lower end to the sternum and clavicle.

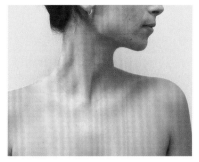

Neck extensor in a woman.

Neck extensor in a man.

Trapezoid in a woman.

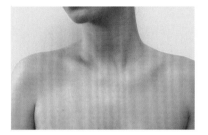

Trapezoid in a man.

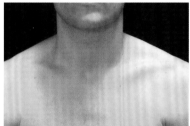

Together the trapezoids form a diamond shape which extends down the spine.

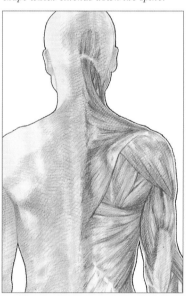

The Trapezoid

This is the thick layer of muscle which extends between the base of the skull, the spine and the shoulder blade. It begins at the occipital region and runs down the spinal column to the tenth vertebra. From there it reaches sideways over the shoulder blade, where it attaches at three points: to the outside of the collar bone; to the outer ridge of the shoulder blade (the acromion), and to the inner side of this same top ridge. Together the two trapezoids build a sheet of muscle which stretches down the back. The space between the two tendons at the top of the neck forms the nape; this is more pronounced in children and often covered by hair. The upper edge of the trapezoid defines the contour of

the lower neck.

Between the collar bone, neck and trapezoid lies the triangular depression sometimes known as the salt cellar – a feature to be observed but not overemphasised. Study the photographs on this page closely and familiarise yourself with the interrelation of the shoulder girdle, neck and trapezoid muscles.

The Throat

The region we generally call the 'throat' lies between the two extensor muscles at the front of the neck. This area shelters the windpipe and the larynx and pharynx, and is covered by various muscle groups, including those of the upper and lower tongue. But we need not investigate the throat

in such great detail. What is important to note, however, is the extent to which the Adam's apple (thyroid cartilage) stands out in a man, while in a woman it forms only a light swelling on the surface of the neck. At the point where it meets the top of the collar bone, the throat 'disappears' inwards, forming the slight hollow sometimes called the jugular.

17

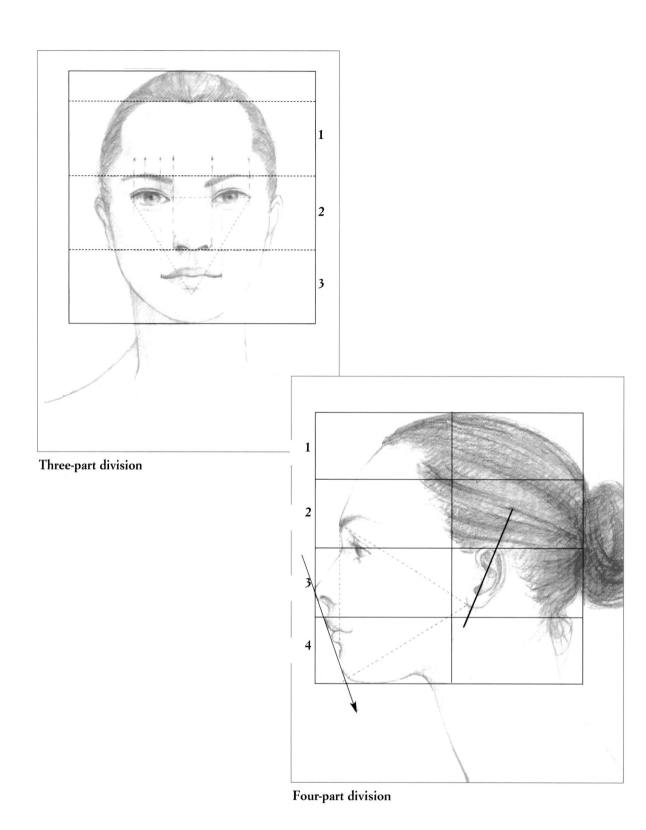

Three-part division

Four-part division

Proportions of the head and neck

18

3 *The Head and its Proportions*

Although it is true that each individual is unique, nonetheless when it comes to the shape of the head, there exist more similarities than differences. Let us examine two alternative rules, both of which will assist you in structuring your approach to the modelling of the head and face.

On the one hand, it is possible to divide the face into three equal parts. The upper part extends from the hair line to the eyebrow; the middle part from the eyebrow to just beneath the nose, and the third from here to the chin. Equally possible – and, moreover, more interesting – is the division of the whole head into two equal halves. In adults the dividing line between the two halves of the head (from the underside of the chin to the crown of the skull) runs horizontally through the centre of the eyes. This middle line can shift up or down marginally depending on the length of a face, but it never lies outside the eye zone. If we divide the lower half of the head into two further sections, we will find a point that lies just above the upper lip. Joining the points at the outer corner of each eye with the middle point of the lower lip, we can describe an equilateral triangle (see diagram).

There is an old rule which decrees there to be 'an eye between the eyes'. Equally, you can remember that the distance between the inner corners of the eyes is the same as the width of the nose at the outer extent of the nostrils. The corners of the mouth lie directly in line with the inner edge of the iris when the eyes are gazing forwards. The width of the face at the height of the cheekbones measures two thirds of the head's total height.

Seen in profile, the head will fit into a square, its total height being equivalent to the distance between the tip of the nose and the back of the head. If we halve this distance, we arrive at the jaw arch, where the mandible meets the earlobe. The point at which the upper ear attaches to the face lines up with the centre of the eye, and the upper section of the outer ear will lie just above this line. If, staying with the profile, we join up the chin with the jaw arch, and the central dimple between the forehead and the nose, we find we have another equilateral triangle.

Bear in mind that placing the eyes above the middle line has the effect of making the face appear older, whereas the opposite will make the face look more childlike. The most common mistake when interpreting proportions consists in placing the eyes too high. There are two possible reasons for this: firstly, we are often unfamiliar with the true size of the head (remember that the skull does not end at the hairline); and, secondly, we tend to treat the eyes with greater importance than the forehead and upper skull area.

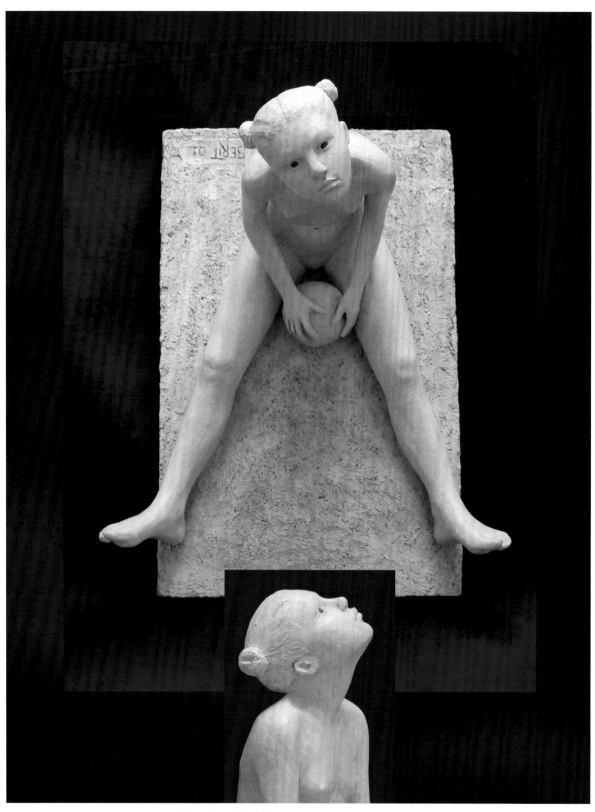

Little Girl with Ball, 2001, fired and waxed clay, h: 20cm.

4 In Practice – How to Model a Head

Before embarking on the modelling of your own head, first take time to observe (and criticise) a few examples of heads produced by beginners in the modelling and sculpting process. At this point I would like to thank those students who were so kind as to allow me to show their very first attempts. Don't forget that these heads were modelled without any help or advice, and the purpose of illustrating them here is purely to show the mistakes and mishaps to which we are all prone when starting out.

As a rule, the beginner has a tendency to rush into the details, assuming that the basic modelling is complete as soon as the eye sockets are hollowed out, a basic nose is formed and two rolls have been applied for the lips. At this point, he or she launches straight into the fine detail. The examples below illustrate very clearly why there is no sense whatsoever in progressing with the detail until the basic shape of the head is satisfactory.

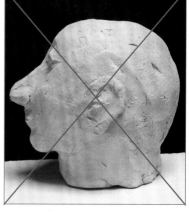
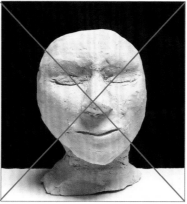
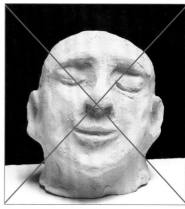

What strikes us immediately about these four heads is the absence of a cranium and forehead; the face takes up all available space. Mistakes such as these arise due to a lack of observation and a failure to proceed methodically when modelling the basic shape of the head.

Modelling a head

1. First find the general shape, a slight oval.

2. Leave the front flat for the time being.

3. Model the chin in the form of a horse shoe.

4. Draw in the middle line.

The facial details will be handled in a separate chapter.

5. *This line runs though the middle of the eyes. Press in the eye sockets.*

6. *Set on the nose and a small roll of clay for the mouth.*

7. *In profile.*

8. *Join these elements on to the face.*

9. *Smooth off the corners of the mouth. The mouth 'emerges from the cheeks'.*

10. *The face is beginning to take shape.*

11. *Set on the eyebrows, forming the upper edge of the eye sockets as you go.*

12. *Remove a little clay at the temples.*

13. *Set on the cheek bones.*

14. *The zygomatic arch extends as far as the ear.*

15. *The added pieces of clay must be blended into the whole structure.*

16. *Check that your forehead also has the correct rounded form.*

17. *The hatched lines serve to emphasise the interplay of the different volumes in the area of the forehead, temples and cheekbones.*

18. *Check the symmetry of your head by drawing a middle axis, or with the help of a mirror (see photo 33).*

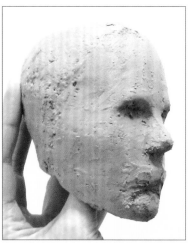

19. *Set on the chin muscle.*

20. *Positioning the ears. The correct spot lies at the middle line of the head where it cuts across the temple, with the upper part of the auricle extending slightly above this line. The vertical line marks the hinge of the jaw and the position of the earlobe. Notice how the ear is angled backwards from this line.*

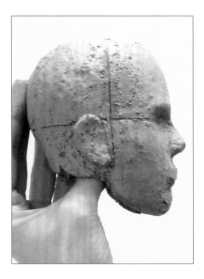

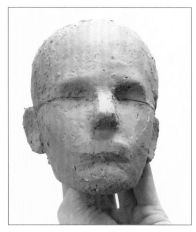

21. *Once the ears are set in place the head takes on a completely different look.*

22. *The ears do not lie flat against the head.*

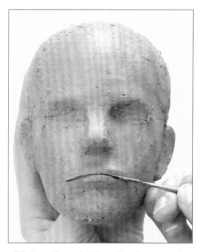

23. *Inscribe a dividing line between the lips (the mouth line).*

24. *Continue to model the mouth according to the instructions on pages 35–7.*

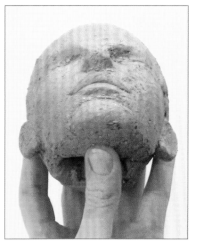

25. *Check the curvature of the mouth.*

26. *Next we move on to the nose.*

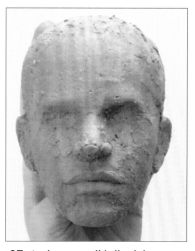

27. *Apply two small balls of clay to form the nostrils.*

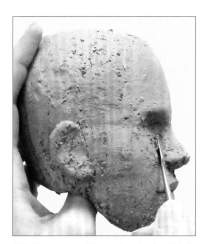

28. *If necessary, flatten the cheeks slightly in order to make the nose stand out more.*

29. *Model the nostrils, septum and nostril walls as indicated on page 33.*

30. *The width of the nose determines the position of the inner corners of the eyes. Begin by drawing in the line of the upper eyelid, pushing the clay slightly upwards as you go. See instructions on pages 42–6.*

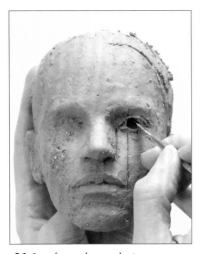

31. *In a forward gaze, the inner corner of the iris lies directly above the corner of the mouth.*

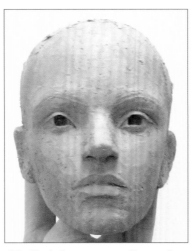

32. *Check the eyes repeatedly in order to ensure they are identical.*

33. *Check the symmetry of your head with the 'mirror test'.*

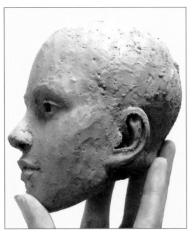

34. *Now model the ears - more on this on page 31.*

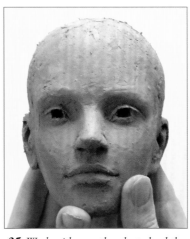

35. *Work with your thumbs to lend the face a gentle expression.*

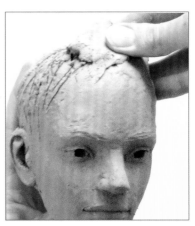

36. *Prepare the scalp area by scratching grooves into it, and dampen as necessary before applying extra clay for the hair.*

37. *Mould the hair roughly into the desired shape.*

38. *Give the whole shape body and character with the aid of a modelling tool, but do not attempt to represent individual strands of hair.*

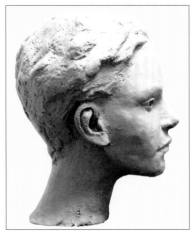

39. *The neck takes the form of a forward-leaning cylinder.*

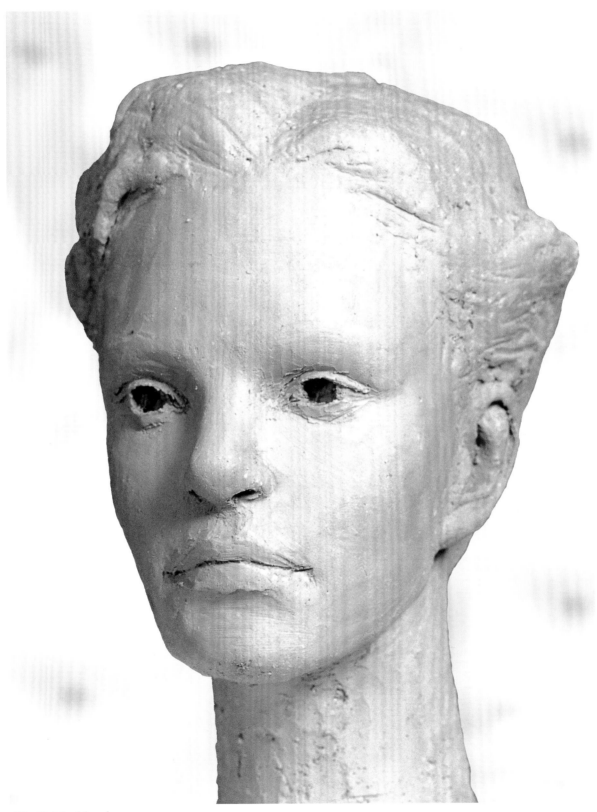

The finished head.

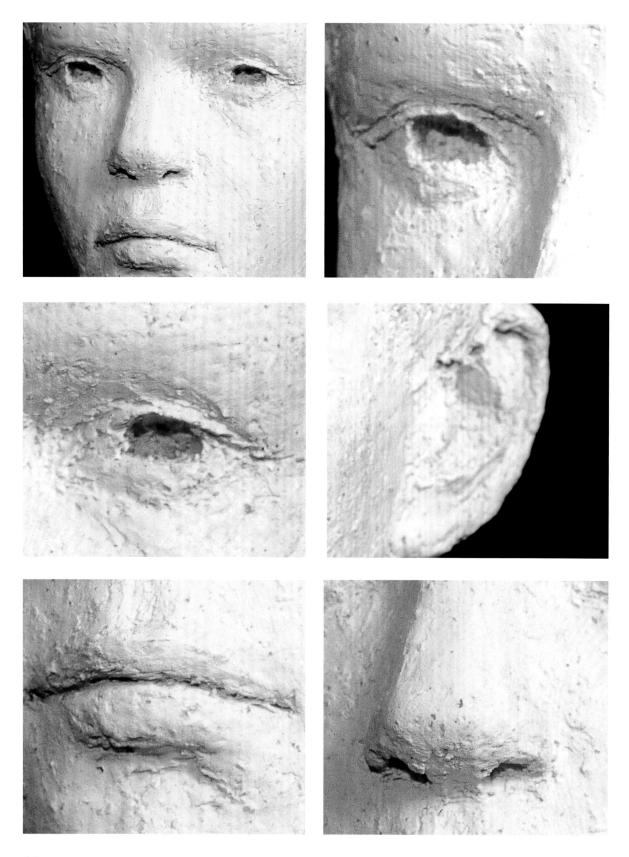

5 *The Details*

Starting work on the details signifies the end of what we could call the rough preparations. And there is absolutely no point in commencing with a detail such as the mouth, for instance, if you have not already prepared its background; in other words, if the general supporting structure is still not right. For a mouth modelled on to an asymmetrical face will always look out of line, regardless of how much detailed work you have put into the creation of a beautiful pair of lips: you will simply have to start again from the beginning. No matter how successful the details, a badly constructed piece can never be 'rescued'. Put as much effort as you can into the overall form of your model, preparing the 'foundations', and you will find just how much greater is the pleasure when you then 'allow' yourself to start work on the details. Above all, do not get impatient. Nothing about the process is simple, and nothing instant. And what applies to the overall modelling is also true for the details: work from the general to the specific; for each individual feature also has its own basic form, a mass, a direction and so on …

The ears

The ear consists of two parts: the external ear and the outer section of the auditory canal. The feature we normally refer to as the ear is, anatomically speaking, the external ear, or auricle. The opening meanwhile is termed correctly the outer auditory canal; a passageway that ends at the ear drum. To simplify matters we can picture the external ear as an oval with a point at one end; this being the earlobe. This oval contains two curved forms, the outer of which begins at the earlobe and rises up to create the upper fold. Known as the helix, this represents the entire outer curve of the auricle, and comes to an end at the inside of this structure. Observe how the outer edge of the fold

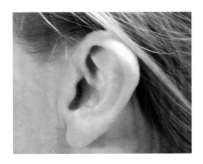

connects to the skin, while the inner edge continues the curve, eventually to 'fall away' into the inner recess of the auricle.

The second curve begins at the tragus; the little cartilaginous projection shaped like a rounded triangle. It then forms a little notch, before rising over the noticeable ridge known as the antitragus and continuing up to the bulge of the anithelix, that smooth rounded rise usually visible from the front. The antihelix divides into two at the top and disappears underneath the helix. The size of the earlobe can vary enormously; in some people, it is barely noticeable at all. The female ear is smaller and more delicate than the male ear. People frequently make the mistake of simply sticking a 'flap' of clay to the side of the head, thus making it impossible to

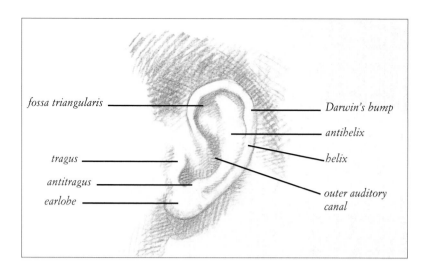

represent the inner depths of the external ear structure. Another frequently occurring mistake is to attach the ear in such a way that its entire inner surface can be seen from the front, when in reality this is partially obscured by the jaw and cheek bones. A

third common mistake is to draw the details of the outer ear rather than carving them out.

When modelling an ear, imagine the form of a sea shell, with its delicate walls and intricate system of curving passageways.

Modelling the ears

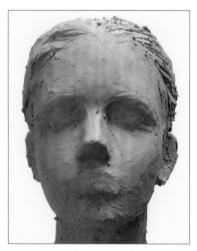

Aim to reach this point with your work before embarking on the details.

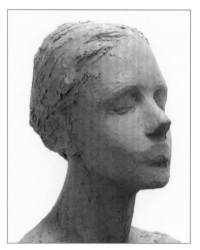

Nearly there …

… like looking through a veil.

1. The correct position for the ear can be found by means of the two dividing lines.

2. Leave the clay mass as it is at the back.

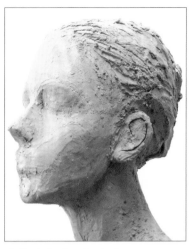

3. Begin by drawing in the outer curve.

4. Sketch in the inner curve.

5. Hollow out the recesses of the auricle.

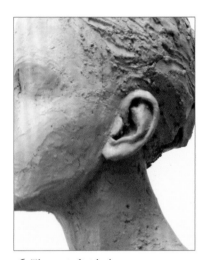

6. The ear is finished.

7. Free the helix from the general mass.

8. Ensure that the join at the back of the ear is clearly defined.

9. Use a mirror to assist in the modelling of the second ear. In this way, you have both ears facing in the same direction and you only need copy the details from one to the other.

The nose

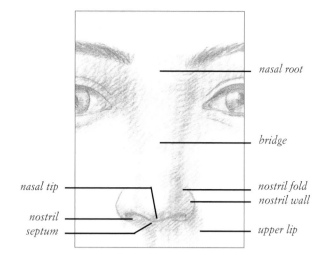

nasal root

bridge

nasal tip

nostril fold
nostril wall

nostril
septum

upper lip

The nose forms the mid-point of the face, and is the most dominant feature. Nevertheless, we are not generally in the habit of having to reproduce it in detail. Perhaps the reason for this lies in the fact that it is not so important to the expressive ability of the face, except for a few expressions, such as scorn or disgust. The nose is a determining factor in ethnic origin: 'leptorrhine' is the anatomical definition for the slim nose of a Westerner, while the broad and flat African nose is called 'platyrrhine' and 'mesorrhine' denotes the smaller Asian nose. The length of a nose usually compares to the relative proportions of three areas: the distance between the eyebrow and underside of the nose being equal to the distance between that point and the chin. Of course there are cases where the nose turns out to be longer, but these are the exception to the rule.

We can describe the nose in simplified terms as a pyramidal block with four smooth surfaces, to which the nasal tip and nostril sides (or nasal 'wings') are attached, along with the dividing wall between the two nostrils (the septum). The tip of the nose is round and fleshy and often represents a light swelling in relation to the bridge. The oval sides to the nostrils are fleshy and free of cartilage. They have thick walls that are thinner towards the front, and run together at the tip of the nose on either side of the

septum. This dividing wall is situated both lower and slightly further forward than the nostril sides. Notice the v-shape created by these and the tip of the nose when viewed from the front. The bridge of the nose is rarely straight when seen in profile; there is often a visible swelling or bump where the bone meets the cartilage. The angle of this bone, being generally larger and wider in a man, determines the degree to which the nose is straight or crooked.

The most common fault occurs when the underside of the nose is represented as an uninterrupted surface, with both nostrils fully visible from the front. Another common mistake consists in not making the underside wide enough and the bridge of the nose too fine and narrow; or, equally, in not emphasising the sides of the nostrils strongly enough. Work carefully to shape the rounded swelling of these outer walls, not forgetting the little grooves carved around the outside.

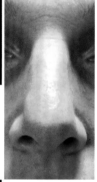

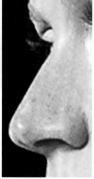

Modelling the nose

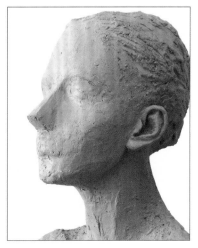

1. The nose is first applied as a basic mass.

2. Four flat sides.

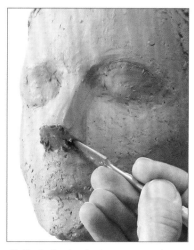

3. Push the clay back to open up the nostrils.

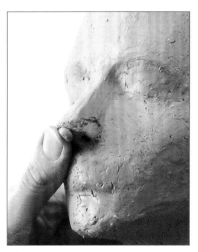

4. Add a small ball of clay for the tip of the nose.

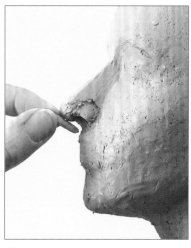

5. Applying the septum.

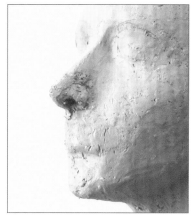

6. Carve out the creases around the nostrils, making sure you have set the nostril walls further back than the septum.

7. Mark two notches to aid the symmetry of the nostril walls.

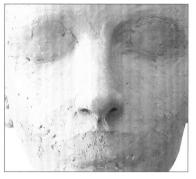

8. Seen from the front, the nose takes on a v-form, with the nostrils only partially visible.

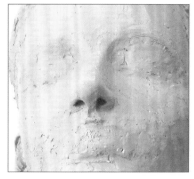

9. The nostrils viewed from below, showing the septum lying further forward than the nostril walls.

33

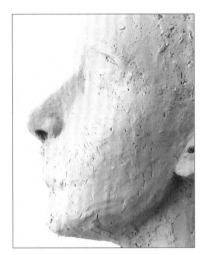

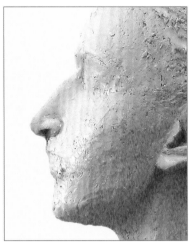

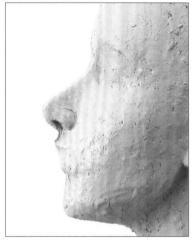

10. The nose in profile.

11. A 'character nose' results from the greater differentiation between the bone and cartilage, and an elongation of the whole structure.

12. A higher-angled tip and a deeper curve between brow and nose lend this version a childlike appearance.

The mouth

In the drama of facial expressions, the mouth plays a defining role: even the slightest alteration in its line can change the whole picture.

The mouth is exceptionally mobile: unlike the other facial features it is not connected directly to the bones of the skull. The lips create a split in what is essentially a ring of muscle, itself connected to the other facial muscles.

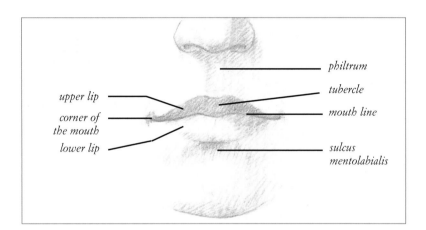

upper lip

corner of the mouth

lower lip

philtrum

tubercle

mouth line

sulcus mentolabialis

The small vertical indentation between the middle of the nose and the upper lip is called the philtrum; or, in poets' speak, 'the touch of an angel's finger'.

The central area of the upper lip, forming the most prominent part of the mouth, is known as the tubercle. The upper lip has a clearly defined form, like a squashed 'M'. On either side of the tubercle the lips slope away towards the cheeks like two curving wings, creating the distinctive corners of the mouth.

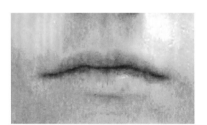

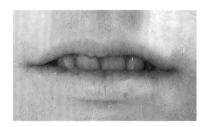

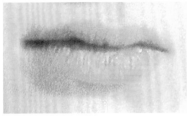

Seen from below, the mouth takes the form of a gently rounded triangle, sticking out below the cheeks, with the tubercle at the point. The curvature of the mouth is tighter than that of the face overall. Since the teeth of the upper jaw protrude over those of the lower jaw, thus also the upper lip extends over the lower lip.

The lower lip is on the whole fatter and shorter than the upper lip. It consists of two rounded sections, which emerge from the corners of the mouth below the upper lip and slightly further inwards. Beneath the swelling of the lower lip lies a hollow, more or less defined according to the individual, which is called the sulcus mentolabialis. To either side of this central swelling the lip merges into the skin, with no clearly defined border other than the change in colouration. For the purposes of proportion, we can set the line of the mouth about a third of the way down between the underside of the nose and the chin. The creases that occur at the corners of the mouth are clearly differentiated from those of the lips and nose.

In its relaxed state the mouth forms a more or less pronounced, downward-sloping rounded arch. This arch is 'interrupted' by the greater or lesser prominence of the tubercle. In profile, the line of the philtrum shows a gentle depression, generally straighter in a man, and distinctly concave in a child.

The different contours of the lips are clearly visible in profile: the upper lip forms a sharper, slanting and slightly receding edge, while the more rounded form of the lower lip appears to swell outwards. The shape of the mouth varies from one individual to another, and is also a determining factor in ethnic origin. For example, people of African origin have thick, prominent lips with a clearly defined edge, while the lips of Asians are generally finer, and Europeans display a wide variety of forms between the two.

Beginners often make one of the two following mistakes when modelling the mouth: either they give it no distinct profile; or else they can make it look more like a beak than a mouth! Observe the rounded arch formed by the relaxed mouth, as indicated above, and note how the corners of the mouth lie below the peak of the upper lip. (The opposite would indicate muscle activity, and therefore the beginning of an expression.) To sink the corners of the mouth slightly does not, as beginners may fear, immediately make it look sulking or too severe: these expressions are dependent on a combined action of the lip and chin muscles.

Modelling the mouth

1. Position the mouth here.

2. This shows how the overall mass of the mouth is smoothed into the cheeks.

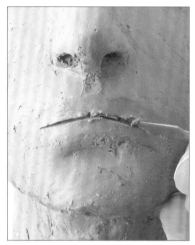

3. *Start by drawing in the line between the lips (mouth line). Use a fine metal tool for this process.*

4. *Push the tool into the crack and follow the line of the upper lip, pressing the clay upwards as you go.*

5. *The rising surface of the upper lip.*

6. *The lower lip curves downwards.*

7. *Use your tool to round off the lip.*

8. *View of both lip surfaces.*

9. *Apply a ball of clay for the tubercle and sharpen the line of the upper lip.*

10. *The mouth is beginning to take shape, but still has a somewhat programmatic, lifeless appearance.*

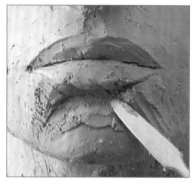

11. *Work in the muscles around the mouth (lip and chin muscles) and remember that the lower lip has no overall profile, except in the middle, where the dimple between lip and chin defines the shape.*

12. *After these elements have been smoothed together with the whole, the mouth immediately appears much livelier.*

13. *Fix on two small rolls of clay to form the corner creases.*

14. *Smooth over the creases, lifting the mouth line in this area as necessary.*

15. *The mouth in profile.*

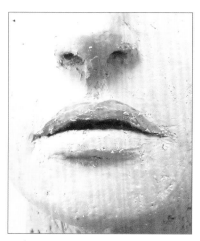

16. *Sink the lower lip a little for a slightly open mouth: the upper lip remains untouched.*

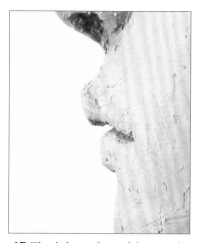

17. *The slight overhang of the upper lip can be exaggerated.*

Exercise

The volumes of the mouth

1. *Begin with a basic shape like this.*

2. *Ensure you have created an appropriately curving chin line.*

3. *Fix on two rolls of clay, one longer than the other.*

4. *Smooth the ends into the cheeks.*

5. *Apply the mouth and chin muscles.*

6. *Smooth these over.*

7. *Set on the philtrum and tubercle.*

8. *Deepen the depression of the philtrum; smooth the tubercle into the upper lip.*

9. *The profile should now look like this.*

10. *Using a tool, press into the corner of the mouth, retaining the slight angle.*

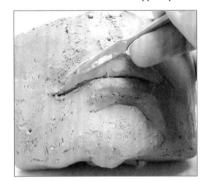

11. *Holding the tool in the position shown, follow the line of the upper lip.*

12. *Repeat this process from the other side: the meeting point is at the tubercle.*

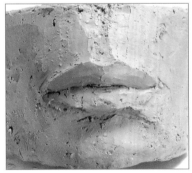

13. *Thicken the appearance of the lower lip.*

14. *The view from below shows how the lower lip only protrudes in the middle*

15. *Shut the mouth firmly by applying pressure on the lower lip.*

16. *The mouth is almost complete, it lacks only ...*

17. *The corner creases.*

18. *The finished mouth.*

19. *Summary of the different stages.*

Repeat this exercise several times, aiming to give each mouth a different character.

The eyes

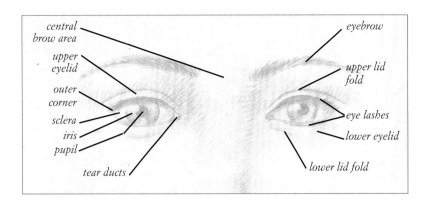

central brow area
upper eyelid
outer corner
sclera
iris
pupil
tear ducts

eyebrow
upper lid fold
eye lashes
lower eyelid
lower lid fold

Never forget that the eyeball is a sphere!

Picture the eye as a ball, covered at the front by the eyelids. We work on the general principle that approximately a third of this ball stands out from the eye socket. The angle at which the eyeball is set makes this prominence most noticeable at the upper lid.

The eyes are the most expressive of all the facial features, and are therefore the hardest to model correctly. A multitude of muscles hold the eyeball in place within the eye socket, and work together to steer the gaze. Additional protection is provided by the 'cushions' of fat which surround the eyeball. These recede with age, giving the eye sockets an increasingly sunken look. The eye opening is determined by the position of the upper and lower lids, the upper being the larger of the two. It is worth noting that the shape of the eye is never symmetrical; the widest point of the opening lies not on a vertical line, but on a diagonal. The upper lid opens more quickly and has a sharper curve, while the lower lid is more gently rounded and its maximal opening lies in the middle (in a forward gaze).

The eyes are not on a firm horizontal; the inner corner lies at a lower point than the outer. The fact that the tear ducts are situated in this inner corner explains its lower position, allowing as it does for the drainage of the tears. For a forward glance, allow the upper lid to cover the iris slightly, while the lower lid should either

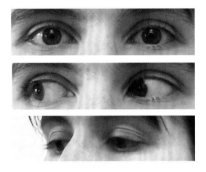

just touch it or else leave it clear. The cornea is a separate, dome-shaped element that lies directly over the eyeball. This is an important detail, which becomes clear particularly in the sideways glance, where the minimal bulge is enough to raise the upper lid gently and thus to alter its appearance. The lower lid also undergoes a few small changes as the eye adjusts its gaze.

The area between the upper lid and the eyebrow varies in its degree of fleshiness according to age. Since the eye's spherical shape is also perceptible from the side, you can examine the three-quarter view to check that you have set the outer corner well within the eye socket (the 3/4 test referred to in Chapter 2). The prominence of the nose bone and the upper edge of the eye socket

increases the deep appearance of the inner corner; nevertheless it is important not to over-exaggerate this depth.

When positioning the eyes, take care over their height and depth. Work on both eyes at the same time, so each effort made on the first advances the work on the other. In this way, you will achieve a greater similarity between the two, even if they are not completely symmetrical. In reality, one eye is invariably lower than the other, or else opens wider; even the angle of the eyeball is not by any means always symmetrical. Of course, none of these exceptions give us an excuse for a 'botch job': a natural asymmetry will arise of its own accord without any deliberate intent.

The most common fault arises when a student overlooks the spherical shape of the eyes, modelling them as a flat surface. See the photos to the right for help in working against this mistake: imagine the structure of the temples, and pretend to insert a large marble two-thirds of the way into one of the eye sockets, covering it over with the eyelids. Also take care not to make the eyelids so thick that they are out of proportion to the eyeballs: such 'heavy blinds' are not what we are after.

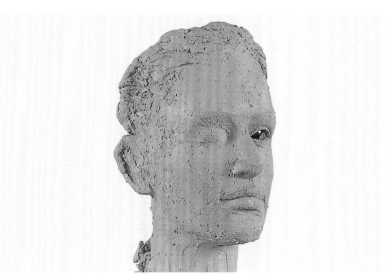

Modelling the eyes

We begin this process by modelling the eyes in a closed position, in order to establish the correct form. Then we can gradually raise the upper lid and observe the effects of varying types of glance.

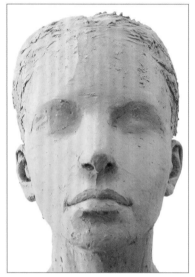

1. The head without the eyes.

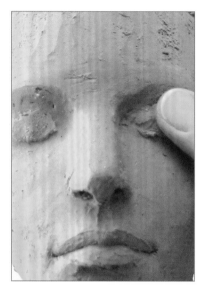

2. Apply small lumps of clay to form the basic shape of the eyeballs.

3. The basic eyeball shape in profile.

4. Mark a line between the two lids, beginning at the inner corner.

*5. Don't forget to form the fold under the lower lid. **Important**: when the eye is closed the outer corner lies at a lower point than the inner.*

6. The finished eye, seen from the front, with the raised areas smoothed off. Observe the line between the two lids.

7. Mark in lines to aid the symmetrical formation of the other eye – down the bridge of the nose, for example.

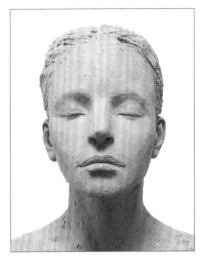

8. The two closed eyes.

9. The upper lid looks more natural once the crease is sketched in.

10. Without this crease, something is missing.

11. Begin the work of 'opening' the eye by pressing into the crack with a modelling tool.

12. Push the clay upwards as you work.

13. Remove the excess clay.

14. Begin the shaping of the lid.

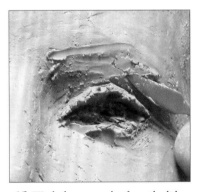

15. Work the excess clay from the lid onto the surface above the eye in order to fill out the eye socket.

16. *Begin work on the lower lid. The curvature is different on each lid.*

17. *Make sure that the outer corner now lies either just above, or level with, the inner.*

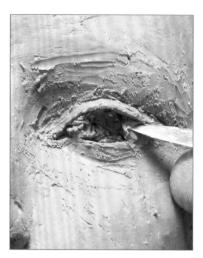

18. *Fill in the whites of the eyes.*

19. *See how the eye hollow represents the iris and determines the direction of the gaze.*

20. *The 'three-quarter-test'. Pay attention to the contour between the eye socket and the cheekbone: it should dip inwards at the level of the outer corner of the eye.*

21. *Drawing in the second eye.*

22. *Shaping the white of the eye.*

23. *Marking in the upper lid.*

24. *Keep strictly to the shape of the first eye, balancing the inner corners and the curvature of the lids.*

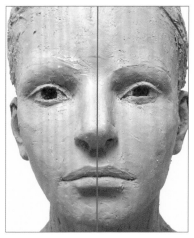

25. *Experiment with different degrees of opening for the eyelids. Above the left eye is squinting slightly, with the lower lid just pushing up a little over the eyeball.*

26. *This photo shows an eye that has been hollowed out entirely; a procedure which is better suited to really small heads. The increased area of shadow gives the eye a very dark appearance.*

27. *An eye that has been entirely filled in. This makes the eyes look lighter.*

28. *Picturing the displacement of the cornea can help you direct the gaze.*

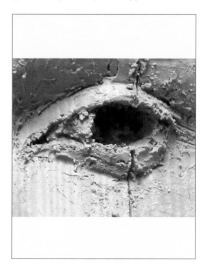

29. *The fold under the bottom lid is important.*

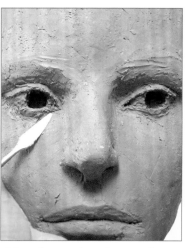

30. *In the second eye the cornea lies towards the inner corner; observe the difference this makes to the lids.*

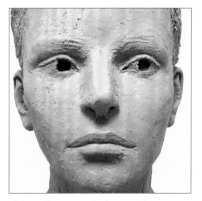

31. *Both eyes are looking in the same direction.*

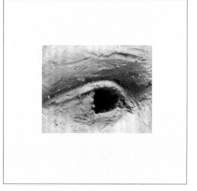

32. *Now there is just a little white to be added to the inner corner of the right eye.*

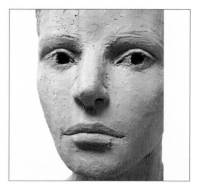

33. *Check the correct direction by trying to 'meet the gaze' with your own eyes.*

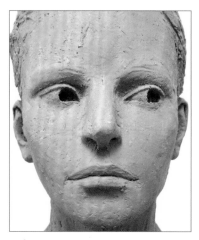

34. *The gaze is directed as far as possible to the side, with the iris positioned right in the corner of each eye.*

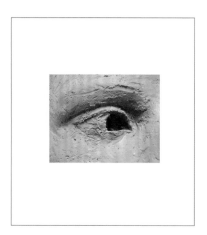

35. *In such a gaze there is no longer any white to be seen in the inner corner of the right eye.*

36. *Don't forget that a downward gaze requires a greater mass on the upper lid, where it extends over the cornea.*

37. *The lower lid lies considerably further back; think of the spherical shape of the marble!*

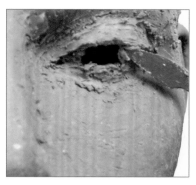

38. *One can tell the direction of a gaze from the whites of the eyes. Ensure that the eyelids always conform to the shape of the eyeball. The upper section of the iris is more visible than the lower.*

39. *The downward gaze.*

40. *The contour of the lower lid in profile.*

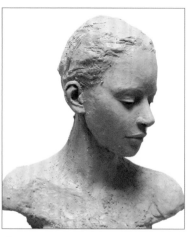

41. *In lowering the gaze on this bust I have also inclined the head.*

42. *The eyes and their gaze.*

43. *In profile.*

44. *From the other side.*

45. *Detail of the face.*

Untitled, 2000, fired and glazed clay, h: 52cm.

6 *Head Poses*

It goes without saying that the pose of the head must be in tune with the facial expression, serving to emphasise and reinforce the overall attitude. Even with no specific expression, a neutral face can take on a distinct attitude, depending on whether the head is held high, straight, at an angle or even in a sunken position. When embarking on a bust, you should therefore study carefully the pose and general shape of the head before examining the facial features. Once satisfied with the complete expression generated by the posture and overall proportions, then you can simplify matters by working on the head separately from the neck.

Remember the golden rule: the head rotates upon the neck.

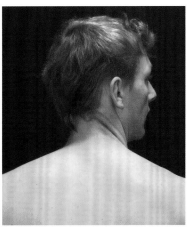

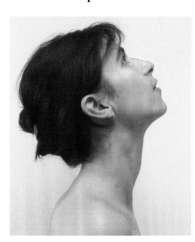

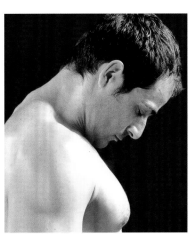

Let's have a look at the most
common head poses:

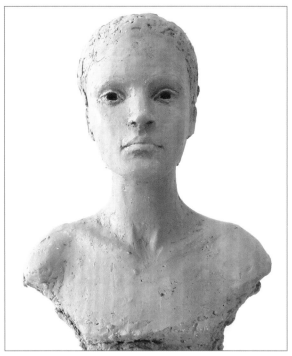

The head is held perfectly straight.

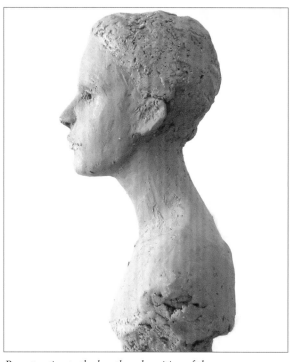

Pay attention to the length and position of the neck.

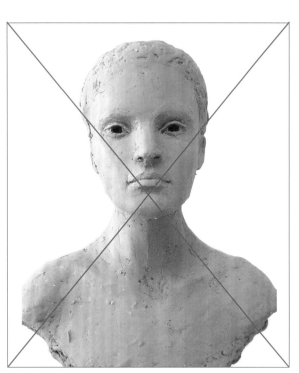

Neck too short and trapezoids set too high.

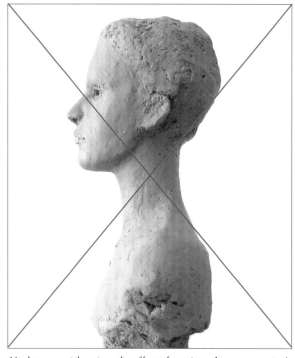

Neck too straight; gives the effect of one 'standing to attention'.

50

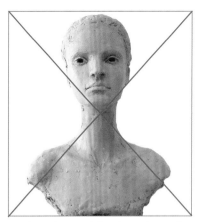

Neck too long. While a long, thin neck is beautiful, one should not overdo the effect. This example definitely oversteps the line.

Does anything strike you as wrong here? The neck itself actually looks fine, but take a look at the space beneath the chin, and the position of the ears in relation to the neck. The head sits too far forward, giving the effect of an anatomical deformation; a neck that begins at the ears. Also, the back of the head has had to be made bigger in order to incorporate the neck; otherwise the neck would have extended over the back of the head.

All this leads to a back of the head that is too large. Do you notice the distance between the ear and the nape of the neck?

Here, on the other hand, the back of the head begins to round off into the nape just behind the ear.

As the head nods forward, the chin tucks in closer to the neck. The space under the chin is reduced, and the jaw becomes less visible, often appearing only as a crease reaching up towards the ear.

For such a position one often needs a support to keep the head in place. To be on the safe side, this should be left in place until the firing. However, avoid leaving it so long that it remains stuck in place.

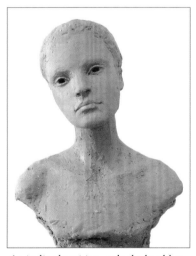

An inclined position; only the head has moved.

It is a mistake to incline the neck along with the head.

Of course no real neck could bend in such a position!

In this photo the head is turned and the neck correspondingly lifts a little.

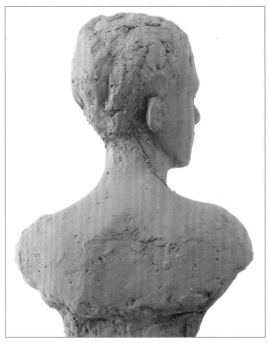

A crease develops along the trapezoid; see it drawn into the clay here.

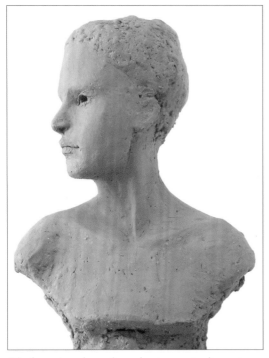

The front view shows the neck extensor standing out.

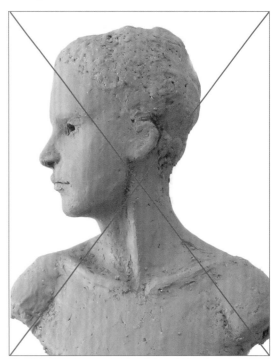

It is unnecessary to emphasise the collar bones and neck extensor to this extent; nor should the 'salt cellar' be quite so pronounced.

52

This position, with a gently inclined and slightly lowered head, is a very popular one.

From the back, the crease between jaw bone and neck is clearly visible.

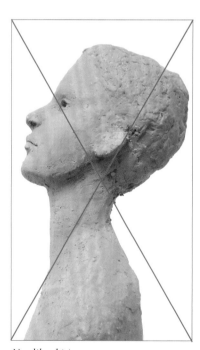

Do not incline the neck.

A raised head brings the back of the head closer to the nape.

Not like this!

53

Attempt at a reconciliation, 1999, fired and waxed clay, h: 33cm.

7 The Male Head, The Child's Head

It is often difficult to establish at the beginning whether the head we are in the process of modelling will turn out to be male or female. Indeed, the first heads produced by beginners mostly remain genderless. Despite this fact, the disproportionate emphasis of certain volumes can often result in a male appearance, even if this was not the initial intention.

The male face has the same distinguishing features: a larger and broader nose; a larger and more angular chin; thicker ears; eyebrows that are bushier and straighter, and with a more protruding brow between the two.

On the other hand, a man's eyes are smaller in relation to the face, and are more deeply set in their sockets. The mouth is also smaller, with a very narrow upper lip that can often appear as no more than a thin stroke. The neck is shorter and wider, the trapezoids thicker, and the Adam's apple more pronounced.

Here's how to make a head look more masculine:

The male head

A man's skull is on the whole larger, broader and more angular than that of a woman. The curve of the cranium is generally sharper, the forehead steeper and the eyebrow bone more prominent.

1. *Consider the characteristics of a male head right from the early modelling stage.*

55

2. *The facial features are strongly defined.*

3. *A male face needs less smoothing than a woman's. Try to touch the surface less as you work. Press down lumps of clay to create the appropriate volumes, but leave these unblended. The resulting rough effect will help to articulate the masculine character.*

4. *Make the nose larger.*

5. *No doubt about it: it's the nose of a man!*

6. *Begin work on the mouth by inscribing the dividing line of the lips.*

7. *Proceed as you have learned to do with the female head, but allowing for a finer upper lip.*

8. *Build up the muscles around the lips.*

9. *We will leave the mouth like this for now. It can always be altered later in the context of the whole facial expression*

10. *Carve the eye deeper and longer than in the female version.*

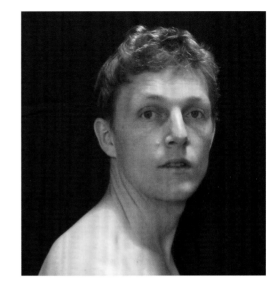

11. *The three-quarter view. Observe the deeply-set eyes.*

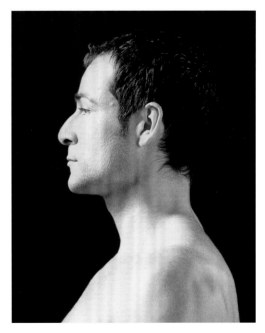

57

The child's head

Anyone wishing to model a child's head should bear in mind that that they are dealing with a completely different set of proportions and characteristics.

A child's head is larger in relation to the body than that of an adult. Note also that the skull, eyes and ears are large, while the nose, mouth and jaw are relatively small. The chief reason for this lies in the development of the vital regions. The eyeballs of a two-year-old are equally as developed as those of an adult; in other words, they have already reached their final size. In the growing child, the rest of the head softens the effect of this proportional immensity. This explains, for instance, why in a very small child only a minimal part of the white of the eye is visible. On the other hand, the ability to chew powerfully is not absolutely necessary at an early age. Thus the lower jaw develops later, in keeping with the rest of the skull. The chin remains gently rounded and the cheeks chubby; the mouth is small and narrow with fleshy lips. In a child, the eyebrows lie at the centre of the face, while the eyes are set further apart.

At two years old, the forehead is high and wide, and the hair still fine. The nose is small and tends to point upwards, thus leaving the nostrils in full view. The ears are large and deeply set, and the chin round and prominent.

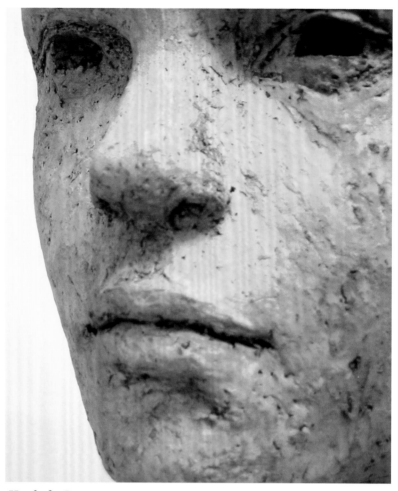

Head of a Boy, *detail.*

Little Girl 1, *details.*

58

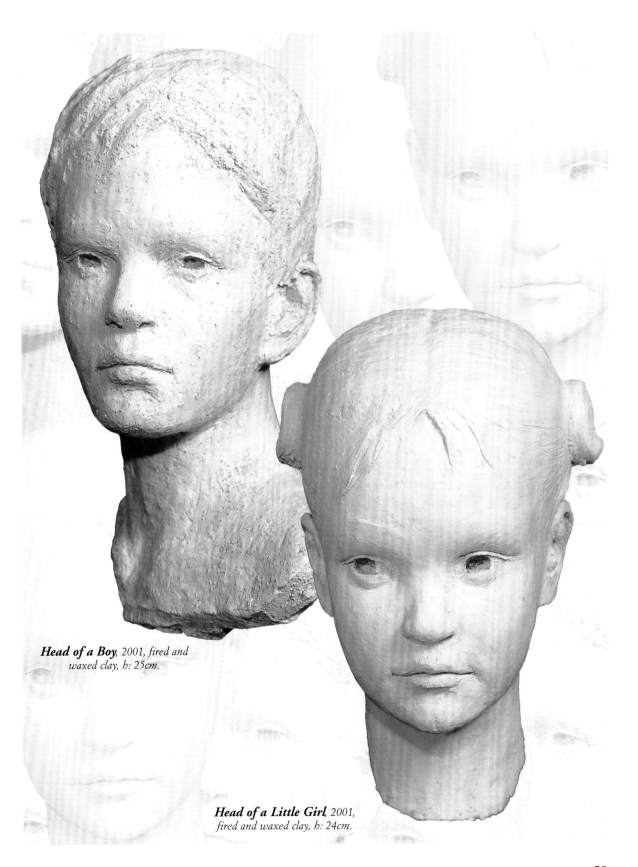

Head of a Boy, *2001, fired and waxed clay, h: 25cm.*

Head of a Little Girl, *2001, fired and waxed clay, h: 24cm.*

Elsa, 2003, fired and waxed clay, h: 25 cm.

8 *The Facial Muscles*

The face houses some thirty-six muscles. We will restrict our study to just a few; in particular those which influence facial expression.

The muscles of the face are exceptionally fine, but so closely connected to the skin that the slightest tightening of any particular muscle has an immediate effect on the features, and can reflect the subtlest changes in mood.

We are particularly interested in those muscles which connect at one end to the bones of the skull and at the other to the lowest layer of the skin (hypodermis). Muscles always constrict in the direction of the bone to which they are connected, and in virtually all cases one or more creases will be formed perpendicular to the direction of the pull. Example: When the brow muscle pulls the eyebrows upwards (a vertical pull), a series of horizontal creases are formed across the brow.

1.Forehead muscle
This muscle attaches to the tendon at the frontal bone of the cranium (just under the scalp) and extends to the full width of the eyebrow. Its purpose is to lift the eyebrows, leading to the horizontal creases of the forehead. If you look closely at a bald person you will see the very obvious line between the muscle and the cranium, where the skin is smooth.

2. Eyebrow muscle
Connected at one end to the brow bone at the root of the nose, this muscle extends horizontally along the length of the eyebrow. When active, these muscles pull the skin in the direction of the area between the eyebrows, forming the familiar furrowed brow.

3. Central brow muscle
(*musculus procerus*)
This muscle pulls down on the skin at the centre of the forehead, and up on the skin at the root of the nose. It attaches to the nose bone at one end and connects to the skin at the central area between the eyebrows. It works together with the eyebrow muscle to produce the furrowed brow.

4. Eyelid muscle
Extending between the eye socket and the skin at the top of the upper eyelid, this muscle is responsible for lifting the upper eyelid: for instance, in an expression of surprise.

5. Eye-ring muscle (*musculus obicularis oculi*)
Extending around the full circle of the eye socket, this muscle forms a ring that lies between the skin of the cheek and the eyebrow. It works like the shutter of a camera to narrow or close the eyelids, facilitating blinking and the closing of the eye. The contraction of this muscle produces those characteristic

creases that form around the eye socket ('crow's feet' or, alternatively, 'laugh lines').

6. Large zygomatic muscle
This is the smiling muscle! It connects to the zygomatic (cheek bone) and to the skin at the corner of the mouth, and serves to pull the corners of the mouth upwards and outwards.

7. Upper-lip muscle
This muscle is connected in three places: to the root of the nose; to the eyeball, and to the cheek bone. These three branches join up at their lower end to attach below the skin of the upper lip and to the skin and cartilage of the nasal wall. The muscle contracts to raise the outer part of the upper lip and to widen the nostrils; for example, in an expression of disgust or contempt.

8. Lip-ring muscle
This is the only muscle not connected with a bone. It attaches to the muscles at the corner of the mouth and ends in the deep layers of the skin and mucus membranes. Forming a ring around the mouth, it is a very active muscle. It plays a part in many different movements of the mouth: for example, it narrows and closes the lips, makes them form a pout, and so on. And of course it is active whenever we are speaking, drinking, etc.

9. Cheek muscle (*buccinator*)
Attached to the back of the lower jaw bone and to the skin and mucus membranes at the corners of the mouth, the 'laughing muscle' works by pulling these backwards, thus opening the mouth in a laugh.

10 Throat muscle (*platysma*)
Situated just under the skin of the throat, this muscle acts in combination with the laughing muscle. It is wide and flat, and is connected at its lower end to the subcutaneous tendon that covers the pectoral and deltoid muscles (thus it lies deeper than the collar bone). At the top, it attaches to the lower edge of the jaw bone and to the skin at the corners of the mouth. The contraction of this muscle leads to the numerous creases that run diagonally from the chin to the collar bone in expressions of extreme emotion, such as anger, fear, or the sensation of pain.

11. Mouth-corner muscle
This triangular muscle attaches under the lower jaw bone and leads diagonally up to the corner of the mouth. Its function is to pull the corners outwards, for example in expressions of sadness.

12. Lower-lip muscle
This also attaches at an oblique angle to the underside of the lower jaw, and leads up to join the skin just underneath the lower lip. It acts to pull the lower lip downwards; for example during speech.

13. Chin muscle
Attaching to the jaw bone beneath the teeth, and to the skin of the chin, this muscle pushes up the lower lip and causes the characteristic rumpling of the chin. Chin movements such as this accompany expressions of doubt, contempt, or disgust.

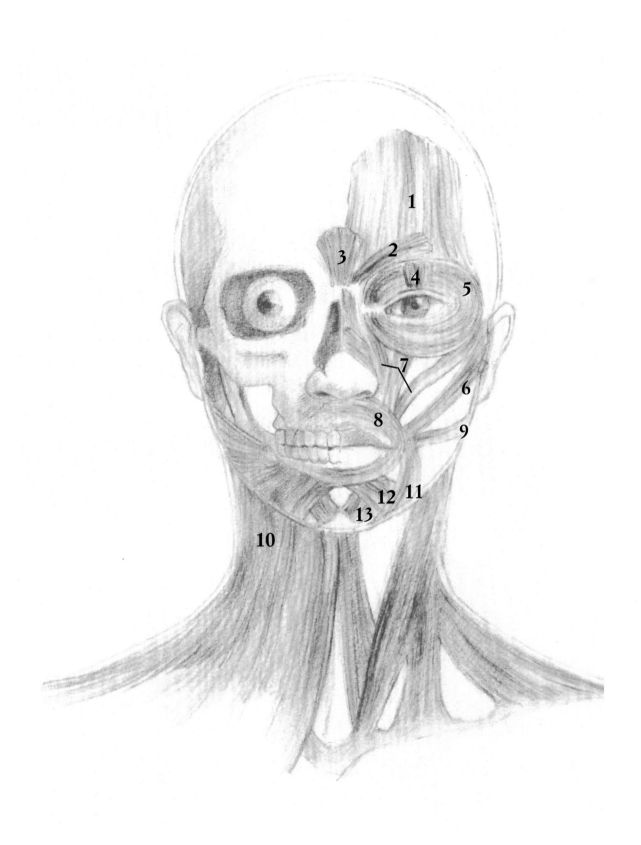

Delphine the gentle*, 2000, fired and waxed clay, h: 68cm.*

9 *Facial Expressions*

Little Girl 1, 2001,
waxed plaster, h: 38cm.

A painter can, if he or she likes, incorporate a subject in all manner of external surroundings. The context thus created around the person aids our interpretation of the picture's mood. In sculpture, such an external context almost never exists. The use of drapery or clothes can help to place a person in a certain epoch, or infer a particular social position. But what if the subject is naked? In this case, we are left only with the person's substance; or, indeed, the being – unadorned and without context. And this is exactly where body posture and facial expressions play such a significant role.

Our aim is to study a few important expressions: melancholy; sadness; cheerfulness, and smiling. (By melancholy, I mean that sense of approaching sadness, or a wistfulness, and not the clinical psychiatric condition of the same name.) The more subtle an expression, the greater are the number of ways in which it is displayed. At the same time, a face that can mimic any number of expressions is of little interest to the artist. Similarly, momentary expressions, such as sudden laughter or surprise, have no real connection to the personality of the subject. These arise from fleeting situations, and when the moment has passed the face returns to its 'true' character. (Despite this fact, we can make an exception for the smile, since it is such a highly valued expression.) Avoid expressions that are overly theatrical, unless of course your sculpture tells a heroic narrative, such as a soldier in battle or the ecstasy of St Theresa, for example.

The majority of expressions involve a variety of muscles. However, it is intriguing to compare the two which demand both the greatest and the least amount of muscle work: weeping with the mouth closed brings up to nine different muscles into play, while a smile requires only two; a specialist, namely the large zygotic muscle, and an all-rounder, the ring muscle of the eye.

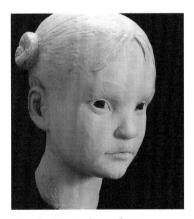

Head of a Little Girl, 2001.

Sadness and melancholy

Sadness is an expression with countless different aspects. It can be an overall attitude, or a gentle suggestion; or it can merge with an expression of unease, fear, worry, despair, irritation or grief. Or again, it can cross into the even subtler regions of melancholy and nostalgia.

Sadness is an expression valued highly by artists, no doubt perhaps because it is the one with the greatest possible variety of nuances. Another possible reason is that it can be conjured up with only a very few adjustments to the face: just a gentle contraction of the eyebrows can be sufficient. (An artist working on a portrait strives to bring the deeper personality of his or her subject to the fore. An attitude of gentle sadness or melancholy can be useful here, giving an impression that the person is deep in thought. Indeed, it is hard to think of a portrait in which the subject has an expression of surprise, anger, repulsion or fright.) In an expression of deep sadness, the mouth tightens and is more or less distorted. In this case the chin muscle is always involved, pushing the lower lip upwards, while the lower-lip muscle pulls down on the corners of the mouth. A face in which sadness is mounting will end in tears. In this case, the mouth parts into a rectangular shape, the eyes close and the eyebrows are pulled sharply together. Both the laughing muscle and the throat muscle also play a part here, and creases will appear on the neck.

Let us summarise the basic elements of an expression of sadness:

Gentle sadness, or melancholy – a simple alteration to the line of the eyebrows will suffice here. They begin by arching upwards; then, as the sadness deepens, they tend to sink increasingly. The nuances in this eyebrow area are many and varied. The mouth either remains neutral, or else it can be altered very slightly.

Deeper sadness – here the eyebrows are pulled sharply together, and the mouth becomes distorted.

Sad eyes – the contraction of the eyebrow muscle closes the upper lid gently, causing the eye to become slightly distorted and the creases at the side of the eye to deepen. The contraction of the eye-ring muscle brings the lower lid upwards and leads to the formation of creases beneath the eye.

A sad mouth – the muscles at the corners of the mouth pull these downwards, while the lower lip is pushed upwards by the chin muscle.

The difficulty in rendering an expression of sadness lies in the many

The face is relaxed, almost smiling.

The first sign of sadness: eyebrows drawn together.

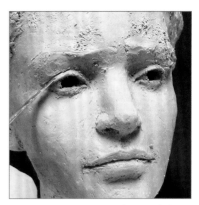

This frowning action tends to sink the eyelids somewhat.

The lines along the forehead reveal how sharply the eyebrows are drawn in. The combined actions of the lower-lip and chin muscles give the mouth an even sadder appearance, or, here perhaps, a sullen one.

Gentle pressure on the lower lip is enough to close the mouth, but leaves the overall line otherwise unchanged.

A very slight opening of the mouth gives the effect of one overcome by emotion.

This face displays a gentle melancholy.

The expression is created through the eyebrows. If you cover the eyes, you will see that the mouth is in a neutral pose.

Here, on the other hand, the mouth is slightly altered. It seems to have been shut with greater intent, and the lower lip is a little raised. Nonetheless, the mouth line is still unchanged, and the corners are not drawn down.

different nuances. If you exaggerate the signs you end up with an expression closer to physical suffering. It is worth working hesitantly towards the desired outcome, and knowing when to stop. It is all too easy, when attempting to 'perfect' one minor aspect, for the slightest alteration to result in the complete loss of subtlety in the whole expression.

Serenity

The word 'serenity' comes from the Latin 'serenus', meaning clear; pure; peaceful. We can interpret it as 'a sign of peace and inner quiet'.

Peace and quiet; tranquillity; being relaxed and at ease; happy; calm … these are the words we associate with a state of serenity. In modelling terms they mean, in total, a relaxed face. No muscles are active; there is no movement. And here is precisely where the difficulty lies: the face may be relaxed, but it is by no means

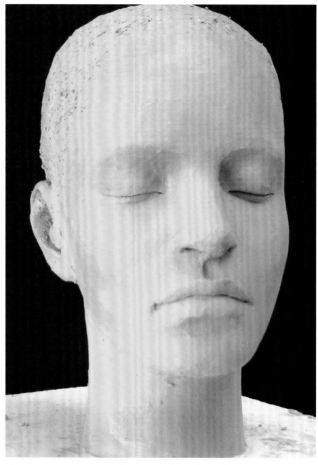

A relaxed face, mouth and eyes closed: all these elements indicate an inward-looking, meditative state.

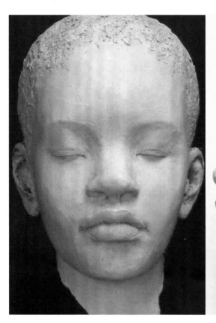
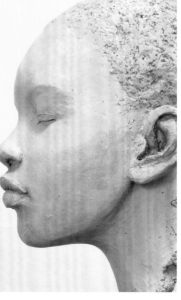

without expression! Indeed, a state of serenity indicates an 'animated' being; animated by peace and clarity, without a trace of trouble. It suggests a certain well-being, or even wisdom; a person in harmony with the inner self and the surrounding universe.

This expression has a calming effect, stimulating reflection, meditation, and deep thoughts. The god Buddha – being the very personification of serenity – is often portrayed with the faintest smile just visible on his lips: a

Head of an African Girl, *2003, fired and waxed clay, h: 17cm.*

68

happy serenity, so to speak. And so we see how the essential element of this expression lies in the line of the mouth. Being closed but not drooping, the mouth transmits a delicate certainty.

In order to portray such a delicate smile, all you need to do is to draw the corners of the mouth slightly upwards. Closed eyes work particularly well with this expression, since they can suggest a rich inner life. Of course, the whole look is just as effective with the eyes open. In all cases however the eyes must be relaxed, with no trace of muscle tension. The chief difficulty lies in the fine distinction between an expressionless or empty face, and one with an expression of depth and serenity.

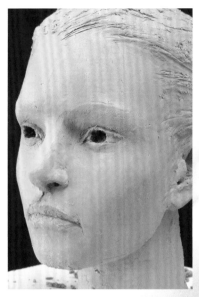

In this face the mouth is similar to the one in the previous example, the difference being that the eyes are open, thus removing the meditative effect.

Smiling

The smile is the one expression which best overcomes all cultural and linguistic barriers. It is recognised and valued worldwide: so highly valued in fact, that it can easily become a mask which we wear in public. Consider in this context its employment in the advertising industry.

We have observed how the cheek muscle is central to laughter. However, it is not alone capable of producing a genuine smile. If we smile only with the mouth, then the effect is false, forced or calculated. For a true, spontaneous smile the eye-ring muscles come into play, creating an immediate series of creases around the eyes. But even here it is possible to crease up the eyes deliberately, producing an effect quite different to the genuinely spontaneous expression. Furthermore – and then enough

of the forced smile – be aware that the bottom teeth are never revealed in a genuine smile: this would entail the contraction of the 'laughing muscle', which is not activated for a natural smile.

For a basic smile, the eyebrows do not contract. If, on the other hand, we add in the

expressive capacity of the eyebrows, we open up a huge variety of possible smiling expressions. A smile can be complex; doubtful; expectant; profound, and so on. In fact, the smile is the expression which employs the greatest possible alterations in the facial muscles.

69

Laughing

The laugh, which develops from a broad smile as the mouth opens further, creates stronger creases around the eyes, or else causes them to close altogether. The cheek muscle draws the corners of the mouth up and back, causing the cheeks to rise and widen over the cheekbones. The mouth forms a straight line, becoming flatter and pressing against the upper teeth. The stronger the smile, the deeper are the corners of the mouth. The groove between nose and upper lip deepens and frames the smile by extending to the chin, which itself becomes broader and tighter. The eye-ring muscles contract further to create the deep lines known as 'crows' feet'. The upper eyelids close a little, and the lower lids rise up, forming a deep fold under a little pocket.

The laugh is a fleeting expression which transforms the face considerably. For this reason it is not often portrayed in works of art. The smile on the other hand brightens a face up without distorting the features too greatly. At the same time, it allows for a relatively sincere look, and creates the opportunity for a variety of nuanced expressions which demand closer study.

The most common mistake when modelling a smile consists in giving the face a smiling mouth without keeping the lips to the line of the teeth. Remember also that some real digging is required to sink the corners of the mouth into the cheeks!

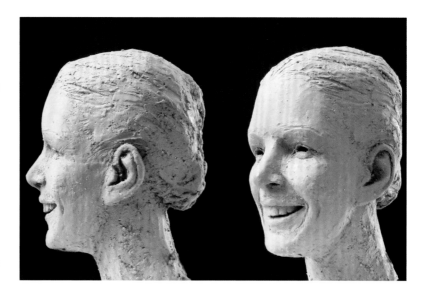

Attempt at a Reconciliation, detail.

1. *How to bring a smile to this face?*

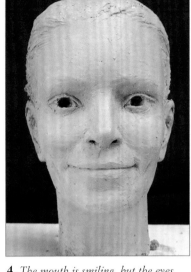

4. *The mouth is smiling, but the eyes remain unchanged.*

7. *For a stronger smile, you can deepen the creases beneath the eyes.*

8. *An open-mouthed smile reveals the teeth. Draw the lower lip downwards, but leave the upper lip untouched. Pull the corners of the mouth wider apart and strengthen the crease between nose and lips.*

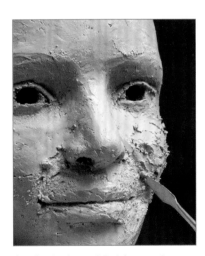

2. *First draw in the new mouth line, pushing the excess clay upwards to form the creases between nose and upper lip.*

5. *The eye-ring muscle puts pressure on the lids, thus creating creases around the eye.*

9. *Notice how the nostrils have widened. This occurs in a grin, as here, or in a laugh.*

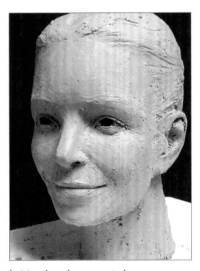

3. *The cheeks are lifted for a smile, meaning that more volume needs to be added in this area.*

6. *Mouth and eyes are in harmony. Observe the now concave line between cheekbone and chin.*

10 *The Finished Surface*

Once you are satisfied that your work is finished, leave it to dry slowly, and observe the following precautions:

If the piece is small or thin-walled, protect it during the drying process from draughts or heat. Wrap it in a dry cloth and then in a plastic bag, leaving this open to enable the air to enter.

Depending on the season and the thickness of the object, it will take anything from a few days to several weeks to dry out fully. Take care when dealing with differences in the wall thickness of a piece! During the drying process the water evaporates from the clay and the object will shrink. This shrinkage occurs faster in the thinner areas than in the thicker, and the variation creates tensions in the material which can lead to the formation of cracks. For this reason, it is wise to protect the thinner areas with scraps of cellophane or plastic bags, in order to let the object dry out evenly.

The simplest method of hollowing out an object is to turn it upside down and carve into it with the help of a sharp metal hoop (see below). Larger objects

Vertigo, 2003,
fired and waxed clay,
detail.

Hollowing out a head from the underside.

will need to be cut open at one or more places and the separate pieces hollowed out individually. It is important that this operation must not be carried out too soon, or you will risk damaging the individual pieces during handling and rebuilding. Test the surface by pressing gently with the fingers to check that the clay does not give in any places. This is known as the 'leatherhard' stage: the outer surface is hard, but the inner still soft enough to be removed. Proceed as shown in the photographs:

3. *Hollow out the inside of both pieces, aiming for an equal wall thickness in each.*

4. *Scratch the cut edge of each piece and brush on some slip (clay dissolved in water, with the consistency of a white sauce).*

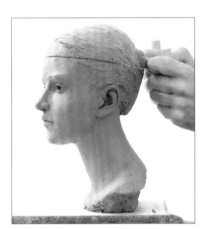

1. *Cut the head in two.*

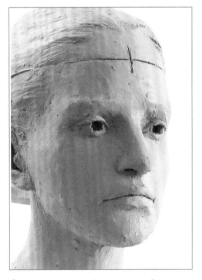

2. *Draw in vertical positioning lines.*

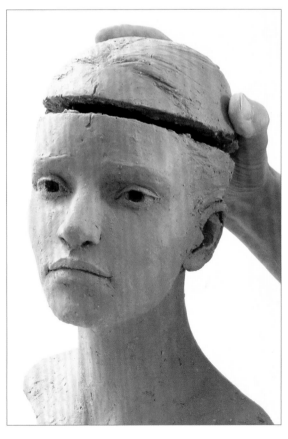

5. *Replace the dome of the head. Apply light pressure and wipe off any excess slip.*

73

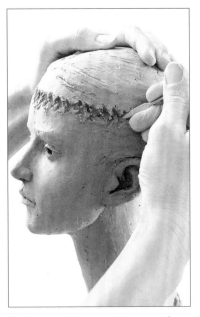

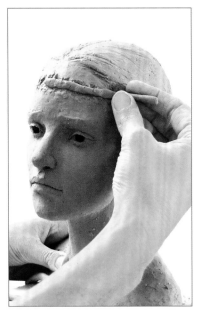

6. *Go over the 'seam' with a ring of cross-hatching.*

7. *Lay a roll of clay in the ensuing depression.*

8. *Using a wooden tool, smooth over the traces of the join.*

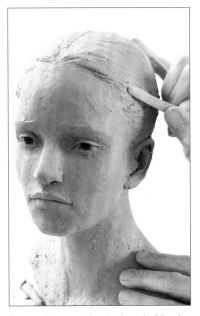

9. *Touch up any details disturbed by the split.*

10. *After the operation: no trace of the hollowing-out process remains, and the work is ready to be dried out.*

Firing

With time and experience you will learn to tell by feel when an object is ready for firing: the loss of water will have turned it a lighter colour; if it is still slightly cool to the touch, then it is not quite dry enough.

Buying your own kiln is a seriously expensive business, and is not necessary when starting out. Initially, you can ask to have your pieces fired by a local potter or sculptor, as long as you inform him or her of the exact firing temperature for your particular type of clay (normally somewhere between 950 and 1200° C – you can find this out from your clay supplier). It is worth remembering that a body that has been fired at too low a temperature will remain soft and friable.

If you are going to have to transport an object for firing, it is advisable to do this before it is fully dried out. A work that is still slightly soft will withstand the inevitable bumps and vibrations of transportation, while a fully dried object could break at the slightest disturbance. In all cases leave your work undisturbed on its base and place it in a packing case or sturdy box, resting it on a cushion of foam to absorb any shocks. Also ensure that it is protected on all sides to prevent any movement. Scraps of foam are ideal for this, being easily malleable and adaptable to fit any shape.

Applying a finish

After firing you have the choice either to leave the work as it is, or to apply a finish or patina, in order to achieve a certain colouring or other effect. As a general rule, any product for wood finishing is also suitable for fired clay. However, one should avoid the heavier or darker varieties of wall paint (those with vinyl or acrylic-resin bases). There follows here, in no particular order, a few recommended finishes for you to consider. You will undoubtedly encounter other techniques and products as you gain in experience: the possibilities in this field are practically endless.

Wax

If your work leaves the kiln with a uniform colour and no cracks, then you may well be happy with the appearance of the fired clay in its natural state. It will nonetheless need to be protected from dust, for which purpose you can apply a colourless liquid beeswax. Waxing makes the work appear slightly darker, and at the same time lends it more 'depth'. One coat is usually enough. Wait a few hours before polishing, and take your time about this, rubbing initially only over the convex surfaces, in order to emphasise the volumes. Coloured waxes must be diluted with a colourless liquid wax, in order to soften the effect. In all cases (and this applies to all finishes), the final coat must always be a liquid beeswax. A simple inexpensive brand is perfectly adequate.

Shellac

If a shiny surface is what you are after, apply a sealant such as shellac. This is a natural resin and is available in the form of soluble flakes. Prepare a solution by adding around 120g shellac flakes to a litre of methylated spirits. Leave the mixture to stand for a few hours, or better still, overnight; the resin flakes will dissolve by themselves. Stir the prepared solution and apply with a brush, but not too thickly. As soon as the shellac dries it forms a smooth, hard, amber-coloured coat that can be polished with ease.

Paints

These count amongst the more expensive finishes. You can experiment with oil paints or acrylics (artist's colours); with inks or watercolours. Always dilute generously, and work according to the 'glaze' technique, whereby thin layers of different colours are applied one on top of the other, creating a transparent effect. Leave each layer to dry adequately in order that it is not obliterated by the next. The finish will gain in depth with each new application. Use a variety of different brushes, and 'dab on' the colour in order to achieve a marbled effect.

Tip: Always begin with the darkest colour, working it well in to all the depressions and hollows of the surface. The following coats are then increasingly lighter in colour and less heavily applied. It is the difference between the various layers that defines the volumes and surface effects of the work.

Other suggestions

A walnut stain can also provide an effective finish, but it can easily come out too dark, so make sure you thin it generously. You can also try a clear varnish, diluted in white spirit. The latter is highly toxic, so ensure your work room is adequately ventilated!

My favourites

For a long time now I have been using water-soluble wood stains. They are readily available in hardware stores, can be mixed with each other and are easy to use. They come in a wide variety of colours, and are perfectly suited for a layered glaze effect.

The patina of age

If a piece ever cracks or breaks, there are various restoration methods which you can use in order to 'cover up' the accident.

Where an object has actually broken apart, the pieces should be refired and stuck back together. In the case of small fragments, a standard strong glue will suffice; larger pieces will require a dual-component product. Once the glue has dried, seal any cracks with a water-soluble filling compound – using a finer grade for small lines that only need smoothing over. Once dry, smooth the filler with a very fine sandpaper and check the site with your fingers to ensure there is no trace of the line, whether raised or sunken. Next apply a whitewash to the site of the mend, either a thinned white acrylic or, preferably, a gesso solution as used by fine artists. Apply at least two coats in order to ensure that the entire area is covered (any open patch in your ground layer would indeed be disastrous, since raw clay absorbs the final finish quite differently from the white ground, and you would find yourself having to start the repair all over again). Once the ground is dry, proceed with any of the finishes recommended above. In so doing, you will experience the different effect which the ground has on the finishing process, being noticeably less absorbent than the original raw fired clay.

Little Girl II, *2001, waxed plaster, detail.*

Sleeping Diana, *2002, fired and waxed clay (example of a finish using a lightly-coloured liquid wax).*

Venus callipyge, *1997, fired and varnished clay, detail (example of a finish using a wood glaze).*

ACKNOWLEDGEMENTS

First and foremost I would like to thank my husband Louis for all the drawings in this book, but above all for his constant support, encouragement and his (unfortunately) justified criticism, all of which have helped me to progress in my work.

My thanks go also to the faithful students of the Ateliers Publics d'Arts Plastiques d'Allonnes, and to pupils and students of the Aubenas Evening Academy, for the confidence and friendship which they bring to me. A special thank-you to Dr. Magali, who loaned me Lucie the skeleton; to Patrice, Martine A. and Sylviane for making their models available to me; and to Yvette and Mireille for their thorough and attentive readings of my text. My warmest thanks to Halldis and Reidar. Thank you also to the models Raphaelle, Andre Noël and Emmanuel.

I am grateful to the model-maker and graphic designer Isabelle Chaler for her patience, and, finally, I would like to thank sculptor friends Pascale Roux and Phillipe Chazot for bringing us into contact with Editions Ulisse.

Berit Hildre runs courses and workshops in modelling at the Aubenas Evening Academy in the Département de L'Ardèche.

Other
Modelling and Sculpting Books
from A&C Black

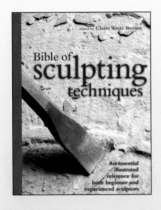

Bible of Sculpting Techniques
Ed. Claire Waite Brown
978 0 7136 8759 0

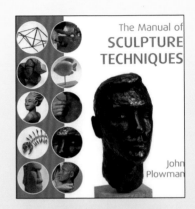

The Manual of Sculpture Techniques
John Plowman
978 0 7136 6580 7

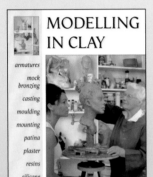

Modelling in Clay
Dorothy Arthur
978 0 7136 6749 4

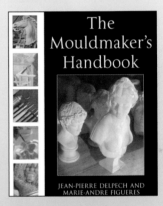

Mouldmaker's Handbook
Jean-Pierre Delpech &
Marc-Andre Figueres
978 0 7136 6770

Sculpting Basics
Karin Hessenberg
978 0 7136 7339 7

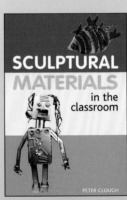

**Sculptural Materials
in the Classroom**
Peter Clough
978 0 7126 8829 0